THIS ISN'T WHAT FOREVER WAS SUPPOSED TO FEEL LIKE

ISBN: 9798277654118 [Paperback]

© First Edition, 2025.

Cover by [Jack Rosser]

Edited By [Lee Glidewell]

Independently Published
Printed in the United States of America

Disclaimer: This book contains themes of heartbreak, grief, emotional struggle, and healing. Reader discretion is advised.

The heart has reasons that reason cannot know -
Blaise Pascal

Reader,

If your seeing this message,

Know,

Heartbreak is not a disease,

Enjoy the book.

Onwards and upwards,

J.R. ;)

Hurt

Chasing them is like chasing a sunset,

Except you'll never get there,

All you can do is stare and wish it was like that all the time.

Coming of Age

I feel as if I don't have a love to share,

I'm caught between the obvious,

> Why do I love so hard?

> Why does love fail so
graciously?

> Can I just for once feel something.

WaLLFlower

When I saw you for the first time, my vision caved
like a sweet tooth.

My heart began to flatter a billion butterflies.

I thought the story continued but shortly after, I
disappeared into a millions pieces and the only thing
left was a broken heart

Misery is what she wrote.

Painful

I would tell you that I miss you but we don't know
each other anymore.

We moved on after and I never saw you again,

                             I wish I had told you I liked you.

                   The ship has sailed but the lover is real.

    So many thoughts light up like a lightning bug and
when you catch them, you never want to let them go.

Why is that?

What Once Was

Adolescence;

Fixate the Image that you are growing old and once you were outside with your friends, when the bikes were piled up In the front yard you just knew that's where the gang was.

Or maybe your hands were wrinkly from swimming in the pool and you decided to crush potato chips onto your ham sandwich and feast without a doubt.

Growing old is hard and over-appreciated, we had it so good...

We've grown up to have jobs we hate, live in cities surrounded by concrete and white walls, and pay bills that are meaningless.

I hope you're enjoying the book.

I know you're bawling your eyes out right now.

Keep going, it's good for publicity.

In this lifetime, why are we not noticing that outside of our "Comfort" there is a world that exists on the other side, opportunity Is looking for us.

Letter

I would write you a love letter but that love set sail.

Little did I know that it would seek high waters and I couldn't do anything to escape.

That may be true but the love was never lost, like a letter in a bottle, it just needed to be found.

Sunsets

A sunset broadens upon the horizon.

Leaving you feeling empty inside in the best way possible.

The gaze pierces my eyes and therefore sparks a star to shoot and strike bullseye.

Stars

Stars align.

        A billion stars in the night sky.

Each one of a kind.

Just like you.

        You're one of a kind.

Nobody else like you.

                Just be you.

Flowers

Oh the flowers I bare,
        They are colorful like a rainbow on a clear
summers day,
                They are cleansed by nature's water,

        The flowers are bright
Life and truth
                Transcends the meaning

Beautiful

        Magnificent

Oh If only thy someone would understand.

Ponder on a story about a time you felt like your pulse belonged to something bigger?

_____

_____

_____

_____

_____

_____

_____

Be Someone

If you're not different, who are you?

Don't you desire to be someone?

Take the time to find yourself some place.

Leave this town behind.

Chance

I still think about you, it occurs to me that you've moved on sprucely.

I wish I had poured my heart out when I had the chance but you didn't offer me a chance because I was the only chance you had at moving on.

I felt used like a dirty tooth brush when all I wanted was you.

We tried again and I'm stupid for giving you that chance because there's another person out there who doesn't take chances for granted.

Untitled

This one means something, maybe not in the sense of
direction but in the
sense of letting it be.

find yourself some place and feel something.

What's something you wish you told them?

It'll be okay.

Magnificent

My heart is longing for you, like a little boy with his fishing pole.

Just staring at the waters and waiting for a bite.

Will I ever feel it?

The innocent ask the artist does the paint match the picture?

Love is a splatter and one knows the real behind the
curtain

Wondering

Is it too much to ask to want to feel something?

I fall off a cliff once a summer when you meet that once-in-a-blue-moon and you suddenly catch a feeling.

I wonder if they ever think about me and if they're thinking that I think about them.

One day that one person will come into your life and you'll realize why it didn't workout with everyone before.

Happening

I've been dreaming of this moment for quite the time.

All I need is to see your face for my heart to shut down and drown in my stomach.

I get a nervous feeling like none other when your around me,

Your blue eyes make my hazel eyes rain and thunder **my thoughts.**

We decided to be friends but the truth is I just want **you to be mine.**

I'm tired of you not being mine. Like she's all mine, I'm all yours.

Granted

I saw you there with your hair tied and smiles
brighter than a camera flash
Flashing before my eyes.

I see the picture and you're not there.

Leaves you wondering how they're in front of you but
not in the picture.

It's the look of love that changes a perspective or is it
the flash before your eyes that once you miss you
may never look again.

Only later in life do you realize it happens just a few
times.

Beauty has a way of being evil in a fruitful world.

Thought

Everything we went through and all the times I heard you out were just distant memories?

I'd be lying if I said I didn't think about those memories, you only have one life and you were an influence.

Suddenly we stopped talking and you forgot about me.

Flushed

We spend too much time giving relationship attention to someone who isn't even thinking about us.

We're living in a world surrounded by people who want our love but use it for their good.

How does that make you feel? Write below; Don't think, Just Write.

Stuck

You did not ruin my life

I've let you ruin my life.

Every time I mess up or
make a mistake it makes
me think of exactly how
I felt with you.

I feel like I'm being
puppeteered and you're
not even the one
running the show.

    I'm getting tired of
    doing this to myself,
        I'm tired of always fighting for it back.

Write about the first time you met them.

_____

_____

_____

_____

_____

_____

_____

I believe for every drop of rain that falls a flower grows.

Tell

Is it harder to wait around for something you know might never happen or to give up when you know it's everything you want?

It's hard to forget about someone who gave you so much to remember.

Name a mistake you've made in the past, will you do it again or do people change?

_____

_____

_____

_____

_____

_____

Have you ever just had a MOMENT?

Moment

I look back on that day as I'm driving away and I can't help but remember your face.

The moment I walked past you.

The sudden breeze of rose scented perfume flushed in the produce section at Whole Foods.

You walked past me as I looked back at you and time suddenly stopped.

I was too scared at that moment that I couldn't bring words out of my mouth.

So I walked away and here I sit in my own worst enemy because I didn't say Hi.

To me Love is just purely beautiful

Isn't the RUSH of your heart racing, or the feeling that you can't breathe when you see them just gut wrenching in the most beautiful way?

Sometimes I wish they thought about me the same way I think about them

The worst things in life come free to us.

Heartbreak is a beautiful thing

Not only the feeling of a piece of your heart being broken off, but the watery drops falling from your eyes and the constant race of thoughts inside your brain

Isn't that just fascinating?

A human can hurt another human so painfully and so we think i don't see any damages or pain?

The scars are not physically but mentally and intuitively

Why do we live in a society where we fall, feel and love so hard, so deeply?

True love never did run smooth

Again

I still wonder sometimes why we ended what we had,
Again and again over and over it replays in my head

There was never an answer to the question of why?

Up and left

Once again square one became my best friend and it's
time to replay the same story mode

I sort of view love in 2026 as a story mode video game
and the story will toss challenges at you, you must be
thinking, When will I just give up and play another game.

False

What if dark clouds showered us every day and we enjoyed the quiet of the west.

The phone buzzing and it's your lover calling and you want to answer but you're giving them space.

Isn't that supposed to make sense?

What's supposed to make sense?

The fact that rain falls when I'm sad and the west is quiet when I'm happy.

I'm constantly stuck in a cycle where I'm surrounded by people I cannot stand and feel an immense amount of pressure to be someone I'm not.

Comfort

I think there's this idea that there's a right person, wrong time sort of thing and we're given this false hope that maybe it will work out someday.

I have some clarity for you.

It's never gonna happen.

and that's the beautiful thing.

We're experimenting and finding ourselves.

Comfort is only nice with someone else and I beg to differ that comfort is nice when you love yourself.

Soak

I know you like to fantasize and think
about what it would be like if you were with this
person.

Not everything has to make sense in the books.

I think we ponder more on the idea rather than
seeking out the truth.

And the truth is:

One day all our memories will be forgotten and you'll
wish you had been a sponge.

Way

I bribed an officer for a ride to Texas. That's how I feel about it.

It feels more like when it's pouring rain and your favorite coming of age song plays and all you want to do is wear your clothes and jump around in the rain.

I can't tell if it's the distance or the fact that we haven't met that makes this feeling so much more broad and tasteful.
Like a michelin star restaurant,

She's 5 star and made with passion, she has her own taste and leaves no room for a word, I can't help but just think about her on a regular basis and wonder what song is running through her head or what she's going to eat for dinner, or maybe she's thinking about what tree bark is made out of.

Mountains aren't strong enough for what I'm about to say but dare I say it,

That I am intrigued by her and if she may see this, may she know that I am desperate to hear more of her voice as she expresses her own art.

Nowhere

I hate that we are initially forced to graduate high school and immediately jump back into college for another 2 or so years, and listen to some dipshit teach you about some lame crap we already know.

There's too much pressure to not wander,

but to be surrounded by people that commit themselves to ungodly things, struggle to find a minimal job that pays minimal cash and feel explicitly stressed out.

I feel like Randy Pink Floyd

I'm gonna end up doing it, just not right now, I need my space.

You've made it to the end of the book.

They always say "Celebrate the losses too" and I
stand by that.

You didn't lose anything but a piece of something
that wasn't meant for you since the beginning.

You had to go through what you did for you to find
that out.

Dark nights teach us lessons, so we can shine when the sun rises. - J.R.

www.ingramcontent.com/pod-product-compliance
Lightning Source LLC
Chambersburg PA
CBHW011232120626
46549CB00008B/3243